FROM A CHICKEN
TO AN EAGLE
(What Happens When You Change)

by
JERRY FANKHAUSER, M.S.W.

Portions reprinted by permission from *A Book of Days*, by Malcolm Boyd, Random House. © 1968.

Portions reprinted by permission from *A Course in Miracles*. © 1975 from the Foundation for Inner Peace, Glen Ellen, CA.

Portions reprinted with permission from *Forgiveness and Jesus*. © 1983, from Kenneth Wapnick and the Foundation for A Course in Miracles, Roscoe, New York.

Portions reprinted by permission from *Christian Psychology in A Course in Miracles*, © 1978, from the Foundation for a Course in Miracles, Roscoe, New York.

ISBN: 0-9617006-0-2

Typography and Printing by
D. Armstrong Co., Inc.
Houston, Texas

Other Books by the Author

The Power of Affirmations

Everybody is Your Teacher

The Way of the Eagle

The Process of Waking Up

This book is dedicated to

the Spirit of Love within each of us,

that eagle

waiting to be discovered,

to show us the way home.

Acknowledgments

I wish to express my deep gratitude to:

- all those people who helped bring *A Course in Miracles* into being.

- all those patients who have been my teachers in helping me to understand the change process.

- Adrianne Rollins for her supportive help in editing and typing the manuscript.

- The Foundation for Inner Peace for permission to quote from *A Course in Miracles*.

Table of Contents

Introduction xi

The Chicken and the Eagle 1

Chapter I
The Philosophy of the Chicken 5

Chapter II
The Philosophy of the Eagle 23

Chapter III
How the Chicken Discovered
He was an Eagle 33

Chapter IV
The Dynamics of the Change Process 39

Chapter V
An Overview of the Change Process 55

Conclusion 61

Introduction

"Everybody Is Your Teacher." This statement describes one of the basic philosophies on which I have based my life and my practice as a psychotherapist. The people I see in my office have been some of the best instructors I have ever known. The story of the chicken and the eagle was given to me by one of my patients, and the idea about the change process comes from observing the process of change in myself and in the people with whom I work. Sharing this process of change has become an important part of my therapy practice. Frequent comments such as: "I'm really glad you explained to me what I will be going through as I change; it has helped me to be less frightened"; "I can now see what I'm going through as a process and this knowledge helps to keep me centered" . . . lets me know the value of this information. The diagram in the last part of the book is the unfolding of a picture of the change process itself.

Understanding the dynamics of psychological change is as vital as the change itself, and the knowledge of this process is part of the support system needed as the person experiences the change.

To be supportive to your personal growth and expansion is my personal goal in this book.

The Chicken and the Eagle

One day a naturalist who was passing by inquired of the owner why it was that an eagle, the king of all birds, should be confined to live in the barnyard with the chickens.

"Since I have given it chicken feed and trained it to be a chicken, it has never learned to fly," replied the owner. "It behaves as chickens behave, so it is no longer an eagle."

"Still," insisted the naturalist, "it has the heart of an eagle and can surely be taught to fly."

After talking it over, the two men agreed to find out whether this was possible. Gently the naturalist took the eagle in his arms and said, "You belong to the sky and not to the earth. Stretch forth your wings and fly."

The eagle, however, was confused; he did not know who he was. Seeing the chickens eating their food, he jumped down to be with them again.

Undismayed, the naturalist took the eagle on the following day up on the roof of the house and urged him again, saying, "You are an eagle. Stretch forth your wings and fly." But the eagle was afraid of his unknown self and world and jumped down once more for the chicken food.

On the third day the naturalist rose early and took the eagle out of the barnyard to a high mountain. There he held the king of birds high above him and encouraged him again, saying, "You are an eagle. You belong to the sky as well as the earth. Stretch forth your wings now and fly."

The eagle looked back towards the barnyard and up to the sky. Still he did not fly. Then the naturalist lifted him straight towards the sun and it happened that the eagle began to tremble; slowly he stretched his wings. At last, with a triumphant cry he soared into the heavens.

It may be that the eagle still remembers the chickens with nostalgia; it may even be that he occasionally revisits the barnyard. But as far as anyone knows, he has never returned to lead the life of a chicken. He was an eagle though he had been kept and tamed as a chicken.

Just like the eagle, people who have learned to think of themselves as something they are not can redecide in favor of what they really are.

This is our story—a story about accepting something about ourselves that is not true and living as if it were true—as chickens. We think we are chickens because we have accepted a perception about ourselves that is the chicken philosophy of life. In truth, we really are eagles with the potential to soar, to be free to experience our real essence: love, joy, peace, freedom. But alas, we find ourselves in the chicken yard feeling safe yet fearful, and with no sense of life, purpose or direction.

How do we get out of the chicken yard? The following pages will describe an overview of the chicken philosophy, contrasting it with the eagle's philosophy. The last part of the book illustrates the dynamics of what happens when we move from being chickens to discover the eagles that we are.

What you are depends on what you believe to be true about yourself. There are two ways of looking at yourself: (1) through the eyes of the chicken philosophy or (2) eagle philosophy. The way we relate to ourselves, those around us and the world, is determined by the philosophy we accept to be true. The first step out of the chicken yard is to understand the basic ideas of each philosophy. Only as we see clearly the basic beliefs of the chicken yard can we accept where we are right now and what keeps us in this unhappy state. Understanding the basic beliefs of the eagle philosophy gives us a choice and also points the way to our accepting who and what we really are.

Chapter I

The Philosophy of the Chicken

As I describe the chicken philosophy, it must be understood that there seems to be a logic to this way of looking at life. Its basic ideas will seem to make sense. The only problem is that this way of life doesn't work. It gives us the illusion that if we keep trying it will work; but the bottom line is . . . we always end up disappointed and fearful. It gives us the temporary illusion that it will last but never does. It is neither good nor bad; it just doesn't work. The following are the basic ideas on which this philosophy stands.

We Lack Something Inside

This is the basic idea on which the chicken philosophy is founded. We lack something and something is missing inside of us that is basic to our existence and from this premise we feel incomplete and dissatisfied. This basic idea is communicated to us from our parents, society, and authority figures— all communicate to us this basic idea that we lack something and are incomplete. Consequently, we focus on what we don't have, and the basic feeling underlying this perception is fear. This idea of the fear of lack is the foundation of the chicken philosophy; and if we accept this perception to be true about ourselves, then the following ideas will *seem* to have a logical sequence. The only problem is that, as we will discuss later, this way of looking at ourselves and at life never works out and is not true.

We need something outside of ourselves to make us feel secure, happy and worth something as a person.

If we lack something and are incomplete within ourselves, then it would follow that we would seek to fill this void and lack from an outside source. Our focus is now on what other people have that we think we don't have. Our goal now becomes getting. The more we see what others have that we lack, the more fearful we become that we won't acquire it; and this fear of not getting is what motivates us to continue. The feeling is that if we can get enough things and the right things, we will be happy and complete. Malcolm Boyd in his "Book of Days" describes what happens to us when we try to find the right thing outside of ourselves to make us happy. "I decided to try them; not everything, but the right ones. Ad men henceforth would be my prophets. They talked about such pleasant things, always on the bright side—except for the day when the postman would leave the bills. But the ad men said, pay by installments. I bought the right car, the right gin, the right suits, the right TV set, the right chocolates, the right deodorants, the right coffee, the right suppositories and the right life insurance. I switched to the right cigarette, the right newspaper, the right vermouth, the right church, the right suntan ointment, the right undergarment, the right new magazine and the right airline. And what did I find? Milk and honey? My image and I are now exact. I'm no longer me . . . I'm it."* Even though this is the outcome, we still keep trying with the illusion that the next thing will be the key to our happiness and security.

Along with the illusion of finding that right thing or the accumulation of things, we look for that right person. There is someone out there who is special and just right for me, and when I find that person I shall be happy and complete. This is like the story of the man who was looking for the "perfect" or right woman and was becoming frustrated because he could never find her. One day he told his friend that he had found the right and perfect woman. "Well, when are you getting married?" asked the friend. "We're not," was the reply. "You see, she was looking for the perfect man." The chicken philosophy says that some thing or some person outside ourselves is the source of our being okay, accepted and loved.

When You Give Something You Lose It

If we accept the perception that we lack something, then it would follow that if we give something of ourselves, we would lose it and consequently

*Book of Days, *Malcolm Boyd*. *Random House*, © 1968.

experience more lack. The chicken philosophy simply says, I give to get because if I don't get at least as much as I give or, hopefully, more, then I soon will have nothing and will be empty. In the chicken philosophy, to give anything implies that we will have to do without it.

This perception leads to one of the mistaken characteristics of love—sacrifice. When we associate giving with sacrifice, we give only because we believe that we are somehow getting something better and, therefore, can do without the thing we give. Sacrifice and giving then become forms of manipulation to create the feeling of obligation in the other person. If I give and give and give to you without letting you give to me, I create in you feelings of obligation based on guilt. This is a form of an insurance policy. When I feel I need something, all I have to do is push the guilt button with the words, "Look at all I've done for you," or "At least you could do this one thing for me." My giving always has strings attached because I must be assured that I will get more in return.

The basic motivation of this idea, giving to get, again is fear.

Seek and Do Not Find

We must continue to seek, even though we do not find. The hope of the chicken philosophy is in this idea. If we believe that our happiness is outside ourselves, then seeking is vital to its discovery—

even though nothing is ever found. An example of this point is the value we place on activity. The more active we are, the more involved we are, the more important we are. A common statement is, "Oh, I have so much to do, this and this and this, I just don't know when I will get it all done." We say this with a sense of pride as if this were a badge we wear that shows how valuable we are as a person. But this is just a seeking that never finds, a knocking but no doors open.

Of course we will never find what we are looking for because we are looking outside ourselves; we are seeking and looking in the wrong place. A man was walking home one evening when he came to the end of the block and noticed a man on his hands and knees under a light pole looking for something. "Have you lost something?" the man asked curiously. "Yes, I lost my ring," was the reply. "Where did you lose it?" the curious man continued. "Oh, I lost it across the street over there where it is dark." "Then why are you looking here under this lamp post when you lost it over there?" "Uh," replied the man, "the light is much better here."

The chicken perception says seek and do not find; the seeking is the most important activity, not the finding. The reason the chicken philosophy does not want us to find anything is because if we find the truth, we will than see that the basic foundation of the chicken philosophy is fear and that it doesn't work, and in the seeing we will decide to let go of this perception.

Carl Frederick in his book, *Playing the Game the New Way,** has a beautiful illustration of this seeking and not finding. He tells about a psychologist who did an experiment with a rat. He presented this rat with three tunnels, only one of which had some cheese in it, the rat explored all avenues until he found the cheese. After finding the cheese in the same tunnel the rat ignored all non-cheese tunnels and only went down the one with the pay off. The psychologist then took away the cheese and the rat soon learned it was gone and began to explore all tunnels again, looking for the reward.

In stark contrast, we human beings will go up a tunnel looking for whatever cheese the situation promises, still never find any, but proceed to go up that tunnel for a lifetime. What motivates and drives us is reasonableness and rightness. That is, we say to ourselves, quite logically and practically, "I saw the cheese go up that tunnel and its got to be there. I'm going to find it if it takes me a lifetime." So you and I get to spend a lifetime without cheese, but always being able to explain to those around us (friends, wives, husbands, anyone who will listen) that we are up a very practical and reasonable tunnel. Of course we find other people to agree with us that the cheese belongs up that tunnel and those people are called really close friends.

Seek and do not find. It's not important to get the cheese, just keep going up that empty tunnel.

*Playing the Game the New Way, *Carl Frederick, Delta Publishing, New York, N.Y.*

We are Bodies

The home of the chicken philosophy is the body. Our identity is our body, and because we accept this perception we seek to ask our bodies to give us what they cannot give us.

Body appetites are "getting mechanisms," representing the chicken's philosophic need to confirm itself. This is as true of body appetites as it is of the so called "higher chicken needs." Body appetites are not physical in origin. The chicken philosophy regards the body as its home and tries to satisfy itself through the body. We have the illusion that the body can create, and what we are experiencing in our bodies is created by the body itself.*

The following are some examples of how we use the body to handle our problems and affirm our self worth as a person.

"I feel so empty inside as if there is nothing there. And the only thing I know to do is go to the refrigerator. After eating I do feel a sense of relief, but I know the emptiness is still present." Emotional emptiness is a common problem I hear as a psychotherapist, and eating becomes one way people try to use the body to feel full emotionally. They are assigning the body a task it cannot fulfill.

We stand in front of the mirror trying to get ready for the day, feeling down and depressed. Our hair is

*A Course in Miracles, *Foundation for Inner Peace*, Box 1104, Glen Ellen, CA 95442.

not cooperating so our anger is directed at our hair as if in retaliation for its attack on us.

Using our sexuality is another means of affirming ourselves through the body. In many instances sexual interaction between people has as its goal gaining reassurance about masculinity or femininity. Physical sexual interaction can even become the criteria we use to determine our love for another person. Love, then, becomes based on body interaction.

Because we have accepted the perception we are bodies, keeping the body young is one of our primary tasks. Fear of growing old is equated with loss of desirability, with the final results being that we are totally alone. We need only to look at our advertisements to see how much emphasis is placed on being young and preventing the body from aging.

Another illusion about the body is that having bodies together means we have a close personal relationship. I see couples in my office every day who have been physically together for years and yet their relationship is a disaster. They have had the illusion that being together physically over a period of time will make them close emotionally as persons, and their only reward for this effort is disappointment and despair. They had bodies together but their minds were hidden from each other.

Family reunions can be another place we experience the disappointment of having bodies together while feeling miles apart as people. Prior to the reunion, especially at Christmas time, we feel the anticipation of the family being together. Our excitement mounts. Much of our excitement comes from a hope that we will finally have the closeness of a family that we have missed all of our lives. After the initial greetings and hugs, feelings of disappointment set in as everyone goes back to playing the same old games. Because we have accepted our bodies as our identities we must seek to have bodies around us to stave off the fear of loneliness.

To the chicken philosophy our minds must be kept private or we will lose them. This goes back to the previous step, what you give you lose. Giving and sharing from the mind gives us a sense of vulnerability, that others will take what we share and use it against us as a form of obligation or manipulation.

The mind is always secondary to the body and is used only as a tool to meet the body's needs. So long as we have bodies together the chicken philosophy does not care where the mind goes or what it thinks about. The fear of not being together physically with someone can motivate us to live in unhealthy situations. An example of this is a woman I was seeing in therapy who was continually being physically abused by her husband. After asking her why she continued to stay in such an unhealthy climate she replied, "I'm terrified of being alone and some*body* is better than no*body* at all."

The chicken philosophy says we are bodies.

We are Sinners

From where did the chicken philosophy come and what gave it birth?

Picture with me Adam and Eve in the Garden of Eden. All their needs have been provided. God has told them that they can eat of every fruit except one tree and they are to leave this one alone. They are given free choice. After talking it over, Adam and Eve decide through their own free choice to eat of the forbidden tree. As a result of this act Adam becomes afraid, and from this fear he begins building his perception of what will happen and how God will react to his disobedience. Keep in mind that this is his perception of God, coming out of his own fear.

"God probably will be mad and upset." From this statement Adam begins to create in his own mind that he has committed an unpardonable sin and feelings of guilt begin to stir within him. Guilt gives rise to the fear of punishment, so God is now seen as an avenger who seeks to punish the children for their crime. The God of love is thus transformed into a God of fear, and the peace that is our natural inheritance is turned into a state of terror, anxiety and a defensiveness that keeps us on guard against a Father we believe we have attacked.

So Adam hid himself because he now perceived this Father through guilt and fear and believed that if he let the Father back in his life, he would be struck dead by his fury as punishment for his attack on Him. Adam now feels separated. This false self has been born for all of us and from this new separated perception of ourselves and God, we hear a voice telling us that because we are guilty of this terrible act, each of us has become a terrible creature. "The feeling of unworthiness, inadequacy, and inferiority from which we suffer stems from the underlying sense of guilt, of some wrongdoing that can never be corrected; some basic , 'wrongness' in ourselves that can never be healed."* We are now sinners. This is our essence. It is this belief in our inherent and unforgivable sinfulness that constitutes one of the foundations for the chicken philosophy.

This philosophy tells us we all have a fatal flaw as if we have a hidden closet inside ourselves and the door must never be opened. It tells us that within this closet is the sinful and terrible truth about ourselves and so we accept the fact that there is something basically bad about us; we are sinners. So long as this fear of opening the door is not questioned, our lives will be governed by our need to keep the closet door closed and we will perceive ourselves as basically bad.

Our behavior now becomes motivated in the direction of trying to be good and do the right thing so as to offset this black perception we have about ourselves. The chicken philosophy keeps telling us, "if we just try harder," "be a better person," "sacrifice more," we can somehow erase this flaw. The result

---

*Christian Psychology in A Course in Miracles, *Kenneth Wapnick, Foundation for A Course in Miracles, R.D. 2, Box 71, Roscoe, N.Y.*

of these efforts is that we run around putting out fires, trying not to be the bad persons or sinners we think we are inside. We keep seeking that special thing or person that will save us from this haunting dream of what is behind that closet door. Later on in the book, we will examine the eagle philosophy and discover what is in the closet. The chicken philosophy says we, in essence, are sinners and deserve to be punished.

We are Separate Beings

Because we are sinners and have this fatal flaw, who would want to be close to us? We fear that if we let someone inside, that someone will look in our closet and see who and what we really are and run away. So we must maintain a separateness. To let someone close is to experience the fear of being found out, the fear that what we *think* is true really is true. So we must maintain a separateness and from this separateness is created a painful isolation. To compensate for this pain, the chicken philosophy creates the illusion of being close, a romantic scenario that promises intimacy and closeness if we but follow a certain form. We are led to believe we can be close and yet keep what is in our closet a secret. Of course it won't work because if we let someone too close, our fear of being found out enters and builds a wall. From our seeking to be close but never achieving it, we can only conclude that we were meant to be separate beings.

We are Destroyed by Death

The ultimate gift of the chicken philosophy is death. The fear of death and annihilation keeps us seeking, trying to find that special someone or something that will postpone this final event. Because of the presuppositions of this philosophy, the only outcome can be death. If we are really fatally flawed sinners and have angered God, then there is no way out and the final punishment, death, will be meted out. But we hope, if we ignore it somehow, it won't happen and we can stave off the grim reaper. Fear of death, total aloneness, and abandonment become the basic motivations of the chicken philosophy. Being destroyed by death is our reward for being loyal to this way of life.

The Motivation and Glue that Hold Relationships Together are Fear, Anger and Guilt

Let me use an illustration to describe how a relationship based on the chicken philosophy develops and sustains itself. Let's assume that I want to date and get to know you. As we spend more and more time together, I begin telling you how wonderful you are and that I feel so good just being in your presence. What I am beginning to do is put my security eggs in your basket. In return you tell me how wonderful I am, that I make you feel accepted and comfortable, and that you think about me all the time. You are now putting security eggs in my basket. Now you have become my source of being okay, loved and accepted and vice versa, and now we have the hope that this inner lack and incompleteness we feel will be filled by each other.

But what we do not realize is that the moment we put our security eggs in each other's basket, we become enemies. By putting my security eggs in your basket, I have given you my power because now you are my source of being okay. Now you are my enemy because you are in control of my security. You have my security eggs and can jump up and down on them or, even worse, run off with them. Of course I can do the same with yours.

Since you are now my source of self worth, I must be sure you never leave me or even give a hint of not being there. Our relationship is now based on fear and can be described as "a getting together to keep warm." For a while our experience of each other is very intense and our being together seems like an arrival that we never want to change. Our lives have become centered on each other, all else in our world falls away, and there is just you and me riding off into the sunset.

After a while we experience getting together to keep warm as a stagnant, sterile existence. We become bored, lifeless, and begin accusing each other of withholding what is needed to feel alive. "If you would just do this or be that, I wouldn't feel so empty. It's all your fault that I'm not happy. I thought you told me you would make me happy." These statements push our guilt buttons, and we fall back into line trying to please the other person, not realizing our relationship is held together by fear and guilt.

One day I notice you are looking at another man very intensely. My fear button is punched and my fear feelings tell me you are attracted to him and he has something I don't have and you probably will leave me for him, also running off with my eggs. Panic begins to set in, and my only alternative is to bring you back in line. "I saw the way you were looking at him. There must be something wrong with me and our relationship. Maybe you don't love me anymore." Feeling attacked and guilty, you begin defending yourself and at the same time trying to reassure me that everything is all right. The situation levels out, and we go on keeping warm but still bored. We are now to the point where our relationship is a mechanical success but an emotional failure.

Our existence continues, only now I begin feeling trapped, as if you are clinging to me and won't let go. Because I want to keep the peace and not create any problems, I keep quiet but begin to stay at the office an extra hour or two each evening. A few months pass before you notice this pattern of spending less time with you. Finally you do notice and your fear button is punched. Feelings of my moving away from you conjure up pictures of being left alone, abandoned, and alienated. "He's got my security eggs." Panic sets in and you must get me back in line. "I've noticed you're staying away from me. I guess you don't love me anymore. Your job is more important than I am. Maybe you ought to just stay at your office. I feel like you are just using me anyway." I begin feeling guilty and attacked and try to reassure you that it's just temporary, and that I do love you and will spend more time at home. A sense of relief comes over the relationship; not peace but relief.

If either one of our fear levels becomes too high we can use the ultimate guilt trip, the ace in the hole: "I'm just going to leave." This statement strikes terror to my very core because you have my security eggs and I perceive you as my source of security. The feeling is like a death sentence.

We may continue to stay together for a period of time but the motivation and glue of our relationship are fear, anger and guilt. We are trying to create a loving relationship out of fear and the only outcome will be the deterioration of the relationship. In the chicken philosophy, fear, anger and guilt are the sources and sustaining power in all relationships.

Summary

In summary the chicken philosophy is founded on the presuppositions that you lack something, that you are a sinner and have a fatal flaw, and that your security will come only from outside yourself.

Seeking that special thing or person becomes the illusion of our way out of this condition. The outcome of the chicken philosophy is always the same: fear, anger, guilt and despair.

Dr. Clovis Chappel, one of the South's most gifted and beloved preachers, tells a story that illustrates the result of following the chicken philosophy. It was the first Christmas tree entertainment he attended as a boy in Sunday School. It was in the village church and everyone was there. The tree stood bright with candles and loaded down with presents to those whose names were called. There was a young feebleminded man there, a hired hand on someone's farm, looking at the tree with eager eyes. His name had not been called and his face was growing downcast when suddenly Santa Claus took down the largest box on the tree, looked at it and called his name. A look of radiance came over the man's face as he reached out for the box. With nervous fingers he untied the string and opened it; and then anticipation gave way to pitiful despair. The box was empty. Someone had played a trick on the village idiot.

It's a terrible story, but one that all of us have experienced. We keep searching for that one thing or person that will make us happy. Hands reaching, empty boxes. . . . The outcome of the chicken philosophy is just a pitiful staring into empty boxes.

Chapter II

The Philosophy of the Eagle

We will now examine the philosophy of the eagle and at the same time contrast it with the belief system of the chicken philosophy.

The philosophy of the chicken says:
We lack something inside and are incomplete.

The philosophy of the eagle says:
We lack nothing; we have everything and are everything.

Because we were created by God, we are already complete within ourselves and there can be no lack or emptiness. If God is everything, then nothing can be missing. Our identity is already established just because we are creations of His, and what and who we are is not up for grabs. Not only do we lack nothing,.we have everything; and to discover this we need only to move our perceptual blocks out of the way and find what is already there.

The philosophy of the chicken says:
We need something outside ourselves to make us feel secure, happy and worth something as a person.

The philosophy of the eagle says:
Everything we need for a happy life, to feel secure and worth something comes from inside ourselves.

If we are a part of all that is loving and creative, then we need only to seek within to feel our security and our worth. There is nothing we need to do or say or believe that will establish our worth as a person. Our worth is not something we can earn but is an established fact that needs only to be accepted. If our worth as a person is already established, then there is no need to seek somewhere else for this worth; we need only accept what is true about ourselves. Many people feel this discovery comes only when trumpets blare or the heavens open up; but when we finally see what is really there, we say, surprisingly, "So it was you all the time." We do not need externals to establish our worth.

The philosophy of the chicken says:
When you give something you lose something.

The philosophy of the eagle says:
When you give, you receive and are blessed many times over.

If we were created by a loving God and are everything, have everything, and lack nothing, then our giving will come from unlimited abundance. We need not fear because if we have this abundant source, then we never lose anything by giving. The chicken philosophy says when you give it, you lose it. The eagle philosophy says when you give it, you receive it at the moment of giving. Giving and receiving are the same and happen at the same moment in time. For example, if I express my love to you by saying or doing something, before I say it or do it, this love must come up through me before it ever gets to you; so I receive it before I give it to you. So as I give you love, I am also receiving it. I do not need to get anything back from you because I have already received. I receive everything I give. If I give love, I receive love—not from you but from my own inner abundance of love, so I need nothing in return. Because I was created Love, each time I give love I affirm who I am and this reinforces to me my real identity. Again, I need get nothing back from you to feel okay.

The chicken philosophy says:
Seek and do not find.

The eagle philosophy says:
Seek and you will find.

The eagle philosophy wants you to find the cheese and stop going up empty tunnels. The eagle philosophy says don't look outside yourself for the cheese but seek inside yourself and you will find the truth about what and who you are.

According to an old Hindu legend there was a time when all men were gods, but they so abused their divinity that Brahma, the chief god, decided to take it away from men and hide it where they would never again find it. Where to hide it became a big question.

When the lesser gods were called in council to consider this question, they said, "We will bury man's divinity deep in the earth." But Brahma said, "No, that will not do, for man will dig deep down into the earth and find it." Then they said, "Well, we will sink his divinity into the deepest ocean." But again Brahma replied, "No, not there, for man will learn to dive into the deepest waters, will search out the ocean bed and will find it."

Then the lesser gods said, "We will take it to the top of the highest mountain and there hide it." But again Brahma replied, "No, for man will eventually climb every high mountain on earth. He will be sure some day to find it and take it up again for himself." Then the lesser gods gave up and concluded, "We do not know where to hide it for it seems there is no place on earth or in the sea that man will not eventually reach." Then Brahma said, "Here is what we will do with man's divinity. We will hide it deep down inside man himself, for he will never think to look for it there." Ever since then, the legend concludes, man has been going up and down the earth, climbing, digging, diving, exploring . . . searching for something that is already within himself.

When we begin seeking inside ourselves we will finally be going up the tunnel where the cheese can be found.

The chicken philosophy says:
We are bodies.

The eagle philosophy says:
We are mind and spirit.

We are not bodies in essence, but mind and spirit. The body cannot create, and the belief that it can is a fundamental error in perception. It is essential to remember that only the mind can create and that correction belongs at the thought or mind level. Spirit, the essence of what we are, is already perfect and therefore does not require correction. The body does not exist except as a learning device for the mind. As a learning device, it merely follows the learner and has no needs except those we assign it. It is the mind that gives the body all the functions and purposes that we see in it. The body will be strong and healthy if the mind does not abuse it by assigning it to roles it cannot fill, to purposes beyond its scope, and to exalted aims which it cannot accomplish.* You are not your body but your body is an instrument for learning and communicating.

Being together in the eagle philosophy is concerned not with just having bodies together, but in what flows from our mind and spirit through the instrument of the body. The only way we really know each other is in sharing our mind and spirit. Knowing each other is an experience that flows between people, and the experience of that flow is where the connection is made. The eagle philosophy sees the body only as a means of communication and because communicating is sharing, it becomes communion.

*A Course in Miracles, *Foundation for Inner Peace*, Box 1104, Glen Ellen, CA 95442, text, 1st ed.: pp. 19, 21, 22; 2nd ed.: pp. 19, 25, 26.

The chicken philosophy says:
We are sinners.

The eagle philosophy says:
We are Children of God.

Now we can find out what is in that closet. The chicken philosophy tells us not to look inside because we will see the terrible truth about ourselves, so we have never looked and have allowed this fear to keep us from the real truth about what we are. In fearful anticipation, let's open the door. What do we see? Nothing. The room is empty. The chicken has been exposed for its deception. We have bought a bill of goods, a perception about ourselves, and have been operating our lives on a presupposition that is not true. By not seeking the truth, looking in the closet, we have played a joke on ourselves.

But look, there is another door. Let's look inside. There is a book lying on a table and it has your name on it followed by the words, "The Real Truth about You." As you open the book and begin reading, you feel a surge of energy and life as you discover:

YOU ARE LOVE
YOU ARE PEACE
YOU ARE JOY
YOU ARE FREEDOM
YOU ARE LIGHT
YOU ARE A CHILD OF GOD
THIS IS THE TRUTH ABOUT YOU

There is no fatal flaw. There are no sins in need of punishment, only mistakes that can be corrected. There is no need to prove our worth because our worth is not established by us. The beautiful realization is that *we need do nothing* to establish our worth, only accept the truth that is already there— *we are Children of God.* The closet we were afraid to enter now becomes our haven of strength, a place to go in time of need, a place to go to remind us who and what we really are.

The chicken philosophy says:
We are separate beings.

The eagle philosophy says:
We are One.

The chicken philosophy says we must stay separate, keeping our closet doors well-guarded so we will not be found out. We must hide what we think is the truth about ourselves. The eagle philosophy says what is in your closet is in my closet; the truth about both of us is the same; we are love, peace, joy, freedom, light, Children of God, consequently we are One. We need not worry any more about guarding our closet; we can now open the door knowing this real truth about ourselves and each other.

The chicken philosophy says:
We are destroyed by death.

The eagle philosophy says:
Death does not destroy us because life is eternal.

The chicken philosophy says death is real and will happen. The philosophy of the eagle says death is a mistake in perception. If the presuppositions of the chicken philosophy were true, then the logical outcome would be death. But the basic truth about us as set forth by the chicken philosophy is not true and because it is not true, the outcome, death, is also not true.

The eagle philosophy says if each of us is a child of the Source of all Life, then death is only an illusion that we have accepted, and the truth is that Life is eternal, we are eternal. Discovering this truth is like waking up from a bad dream that we have created and experiencing the joy of knowing the dream is not true.

The chicken philosophy says:
The motivation and glue that hold relationships together are fear, anger and guilt.

The eagle philosophy says:
The motivation and glue that hold relationships together are love, freedom, peace and joy.

The chicken philosophy says my relationship with you is a "getting together to keep warm" experience. Because I have put my security eggs in your basket and vice versa, you are my source of life and there is an ever-present fear of your running off with my eggs, my security. The only way of assuring this does not happen is to use fear, anger and guilt to keep you close by. This is the glue that holds us together.

The eagle philosophy says because we lack nothing and are and have everything, we need not seek that special person because all of us are special. Remember . . . the same truth you found in your closet is also true about me. I do not have to get anything from you to feel okay but only accept the truth that when I give what I am, Love, I receive love; when I give freedom, I receive freedom; when I give peace, I receive peace; when I give joy, I receive joy. Love, freedom, peace, and joy; these are the source of the flowing bond that makes us One.

With the eagle philosophy we do not look into empty boxes because we will not be looking outside ourselves for who we are; we will be looking in the right place, our own inner closet.

Summary

Let me summarize these two philosophies with a simple illustration by Stewart Emery in his book, *Actualizations*. Because we have accepted the philosophy of the chicken, we perceive ourselves as sitting inside a fort we have created, and we are being attacked by Indians and waiting for the cavalry to come to save us. This is our perception of life. I have some good news and some bad news. First the bad news: the cavalry isn't coming. And the good news: there aren't any Indians.* There are three Indians, or blocks, in our lives that keep us

*Actualizations, *Stewart Emery, Doubleday & Co., Garden City, N. Y.*

from discovering the real truth about ourselves: fear, anger and guilt. All we need do is move these blocks out of the way and we will find what is waiting to be discovered; that in essence we are Love, Freedom, Peace and Joy—Children of God and all One.

Chapter III

How the Chicken Discovered He was an Eagle

Now that we have some idea of why the eagle was in the chicken yard, let's move on to see how he was able to rediscover who and what he really was. The story gives us some clues about the change process which will be discussed in general terms at this time. The next chapter will describe the step-by-step process we go through in changing perception.

The first thing the eagle needed was someone who was able to see beyond the limited perception he had of himself. The naturalist in our story saw the eagle for what he really was. The story goes . . "Gently the naturalist took the eagle in his arms and said, 'You belong to the sky and not to the earth. Stretch forth your wings and fly.'" Not only does the eagle need a guide to see beyond his limited vision of himself but a guide who is gentle, who quietly suggests the real truth, "you can fly."

Now the eagle must make a move, a move of trust. The naturalist cannot do anything without the trust and effort of the eagle. He must be willing to jump upon the naturalist's arm, at least entertaining the idea that what he is being told

might be true; and even though he jumps back down
into the chicken yard, he is beginning to make the
effort. The eagle must be gently guided and
supported out of his false perception of himself; he
cannot do it by himself. The following story
illustrates this point.

. . . There was a man who had just died and was
reviewing the footsteps that he had taken in his life.
He looked down and noticed that over all the
mountains and difficult places he had traveled there
was one set of footprints. But over the plains and
down the hills there were two sets of footprints, as
if someone had walked by his side. He turned to
Jesus and said, "There is something I don't
understand. Why is it that down the hills and over
the smooth and easy places you have walked by my
side, but over the rough and difficult places I have
walked alone—for I see in these areas there is just
one set of footprints." Jesus turned to the man and
said, "It is true that while your life was easy I
walked along your side; but here when the walking
was hard and the paths were difficult, I realized
that was the time you needed me most . . . and that
is why I carried you." To move beyond our
misperception we need to be willing to be guided
and supported.

Resistance to the truth about himself is the next
part of the process the eagle experienced on his
journey in discovering who he was. The chicken
philosophy will not give up easily and will use any

means through fear, anger or guilt to keep the eagle in the chicken yard. "It isn't safe outside the chicken yard." "You can't make it on your own," "You'll be sorry if you listen to the naturalist," etc. These statements are used to resist the encouragement of the naturalist. But the eagle continued.

Going into the resistance is the way we discover that fear, anger and guilt have no power over us. For example, when an airplane starts down the runway for its takeoff, the first thing it experiences is wind resistance. As its speed increases, the wind resistance increases proportionately. The faster it goes the more wind resistance, until it gets to what is called point zero gravity and the plane takes off—rising above the resistance. We must go into the resistance to rise above it.

The eagle did not fly the first time but was able to continue through the resistance with guidance and support until he did fly. He was persistent, sensing the truth of the naturalist's words. He was like the snail in a story, who, one bitter cold morning in January, started to climb the frozen trunk of a cherry tree. As he slowly moved upward a beetle stuck his head out of a crack in the tree and said, "Hey buddy, you're wasting your time. There aren't any cherries up there." The snail kept right on going but turned to the beetle saying, "There will be when I get there."

Trusting the guidance and support of the naturalist and through his own persistent effort, the eagle was able to discover the truth about himself.

There are many sources in our lives that can be the naturalist for us. There may be one, a few or many who help us see the vision of being an eagle. Remember, the eagle was inspired out of his condition; someone pointed beyond his limited perception of who he thought he was. We have many naturalists around us waiting to help us see the truth within ourselves, because they know that by helping us, they see the vision of who they are much more clearly.

The final, joyful discovery is that I am you and you are me.

Outline of the Two Philosophies

Philosophy of the Chicken	Philosophy of the Eagle
We lack something.	We lack nothing; we have everything and are everything.
We need something outside ourselves to make us feel secure, happy and worth something as a person.	The source of security and happiness comes from within.
When you give something, you lose it.	When you give, you receive and are blessed many times over.
Seek and do not find.	Seek and you shall find.
We are bodies	We are Mind and Spirit.
We are sinners.	We are Children of God.
We are separate beings.	We are One.
We are destroyed by death.	Life is eternal.
The motivation and glue that hold us together are fear, anger and guilt.	The motivation and glue that hold us together are love, freedom, peace and joy.

Chapter IV

The Dynamics of the Change Process
(How You Get Out of the Chicken Yard)

To move from the perception of ourselves as chickens to seeing the truth that we are eagles is not magic, but a systematic process that is important to understand. In this part of the book we will create a picture of what happens when we change, drawing a diagram that can be a point of support and reassurance as we go through this change in perception. We will be building this diagram on a step-by-step basis—watching the change process unfold.

STEP I. PROGRAMMED PERCEPTIONS
The Source of the Chicken Philosophy

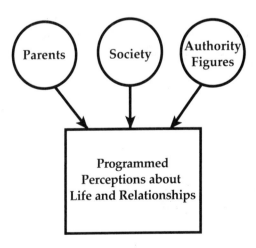

What we are depends on what we believe to be true about ourselves. From childhood we receive input from parents, society, and authority figures that become the source of our belief system about ourselves. How we operate in the world is determined by the philosophy we accept to be true. What we feel is true becomes a programmed perception and our overall pattern for living. The belief systems of our parents, society and authority figures are accepted as being the truth about life and we begin operating our lives on these perceptions as if they were the truth.

STEP II. THE STUCK POINT

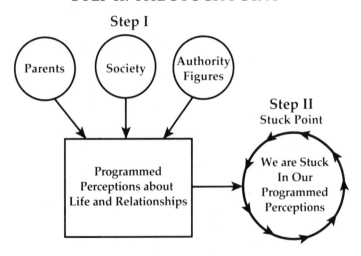

Because we accept our programmed perceptions as the truth about ourselves (the chicken philosophy), we keep following what these perceptions tell us to do in hopes that their promised results of happiness, love and security will manifest themselves in our lives. Of course, we find they don't work but we keep trying over and over, thinking we must be doing something wrong to receive these painful results. Again we try, using the same perceptions but in a different form, hoping that by changing the form we will succeed.

"I can't understand why my relationships never work out. I've been married once and divorced and dated different men (different forms) and I'm still not happy,"—futile attempts to find the *right* form or person. They are looking for something outside themselves (forms) to make them feel secure and happy. The more we try to make our programmed perceptions work, the more stuck we become. We keep going up the same tunnel, using the same perceptions, and never getting any cheese. What we have accepted as the truth is not the truth, no matter how hard we try to make it true. A great humorist once keenly observed that it's not what we don't know that causes us so much difficulty, ". . . it's what we know that just ain't so." The experience of being stuck will manifest itself in some of the following ways:

— Depression that never seems to be resolved.
— Becoming more explosive with our anger.
— Feeling of no meaning or direction in our lives.
— Feeling like we are in prison.
— Feeling of wanting to play it safe.
— Feeling of being bored.
— Feeling empty inside.
— Feeling isolated, alienated and lonely.
— Being increasingly defensive.

— Our lives moving faster and faster, busier and busier with numerous activities, but no internal satisfaction.

The experience of being stuck is the experience of being in the chicken yard. There is no life—just a getting together to keep warm.

STEP III. THE CHANGE POINT

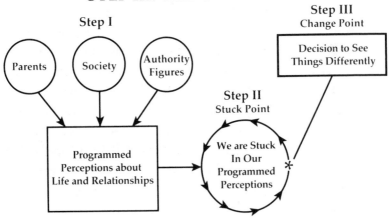

The change point is a conscious decision to see the situation differently. To want to see your life differently is the point of power. Dr. Victor Frankl in his book, *Man's Search for Meaning* describes how important are our perceptions. He tells of his experiences while in a concentration camp during World War II. Basic necessities, food, clothing, shelter were at a survival level. His friends were dying of the cold and inhuman conditions, plus his wife had been taken to another concentration camp and later died. He said they could take everything away from him but one thing, his attitude toward the situation he was in. His point of power and stability was the knowledge that he could see the situation differently and this was the key to his survival and, consequently, the basic idea behind his creation of Logo therapy.

The change point is not just a wish to change but a deep motivation to change. This motivation comes from the accumulation of painful experiences in being stuck. At first it is just a wish to change, then a desire to change, then we finally hit bottom. As one person told me, "I'm just sick and tired of being sick and tired." She was at the change point.

There is a story that describes this step very clearly. A disciple came to his guru one day and lamented, "I've been searching for God for over two years. I've tried yoga, meditation, fasting, anything that would help me find Him, but to no avail. What can I do to find God?" The guru and disciple were sitting by a river and after the disciple had finished talking, the guru simply took the disciple's head and stuck it under water and held it there. After a few moments the disciple began struggling to get up but the guru just kept his head submerged. Finally he let him up and while the disciple was coughing and getting his breath, the guru explained, "When you want God as much as you wanted air, you'll find Him." The change point is not just a wish to change but an inner determination to see life or a situation differently. The Chinese have a beautiful way of describing this change point in their word for crisis. Crisis in Chinese means dangerous opportunity. This is the feeling we experience as we move closer to making a change.

Several years ago a person with whom I was working wrote a beautiful parable describing her experience of the change point. She called it "The Egg that was Afraid to Hatch."

"Mph! What was that? A stirring inside me? Oh, No! I'll just ignore it, maybe it'll go away. Whup! There it is again, ooh! I'm afraid. I think my shell is trying to crack! Oh, please, no!

Well, I know I'm kind of cramped inside, but what happens if I hatch? I've been watching those other eggs as their shells cracked. Yecocch! Wet, feathery-looking things fell out, all gawky and ugly. No, thanks! I'll just remain an egg, smooth and round and uncomplicated . . . I think.

Or will I? I remember that egg from last year that refused to hatch. It stayed smooth and round, alright, but did it smell! It must have been dead inside! Oh! What'll I do? I'm so scared! I don't want to look awkward leaving this shell, I've got pride, same as anyone, but I don't want to die inside, either.

What will I become if I leave this shell? F-f-f-fried chicken? Waaaah! Somebody help me! I could get killed! I might not be as comfortable outside as I am in here. I might grow up to be one of those fat old clucks with a bunch of noisy chicks to look after, and that looks like a lot of work. But then I might be one of those majestic creatures that flies to the fence post and lets everyone know he's boss. Do you suppose? Wow! I might like that! Gee! I'd like to be a bigshot like that!

That rooster has a lot of pride. Whup! What was that I said about my pride? Well . . . let's see, if I'm too proud to hatch and risk becoming whatever I was meant to be, I could end up awful smelly like last year's egg.

That did it! I'm getting outa here, ugly or not. Look out world, here I come. I've got to get on with being what I was meant to be!

Hey, ..., you gonna hatch.

The change point is when we want to see life differently, when we want to hatch, when we really want out of the chicken yard.

STEP IV. QUESTIONING OUR PROGRAMMED PERCEPTIONS

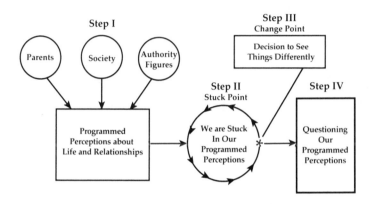

This is the point where we stand before our closed door, guarded by all our fears, and begin questioning these false perceptions. To question means looking at the motive behind the perception, not just accepting the perception as truth. This is the time when we seek to see our situation clearly, to let the light show us the truth. The undoing of the chicken philosophy is when we begin asking a very simple question about every encounter in our lives, "What am I doing it for?" This question asked honestly in any situation will shed the light so we may see the motive for our actions.

Beginning to question the chicken philosophy is to bring the full force of that philosophy against us. This philosophy has been what we have accepted as the truth about ourselves and challenging it by questioning its motives is to give it a death sentence. During this time we may feel a deep sense of loss as if we were losing a real part of ourselves. This experience of loss is normal for what we are going through. Questioning the perceptions on which our lives have been based is the beginning of the end of the chicken philosophy and a big step toward discovering and experiencing the real truth about ourselves.

STEP V. THE WHIRLPOOL

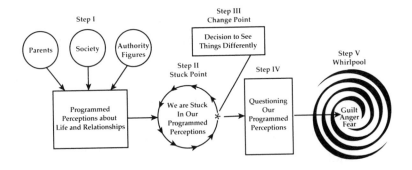

As we continue to question our perceptions we move into the feeling of being in a whirlpool made up of fear, anger and guilt. There are times when we literally feel we are going down the tube.

But going into the whirlpool is a very important part of the process. We must go into our fears, angers and guilts, experiencing them to their fullest, so we may break through and discover that they have no power over us and that what they tell us is not true. To go into your fear is not to feed your fear. The only way you can feed a fear is to think about it and the thought gives the fear more energy. Experiencing your fear is not thinking about it but just feeling it with no resistance. It is important to see this distinction between feeding your fear and experiencing and releasing your fear. This is also true of anger and guilt.

The following are some of the common experiences people have while they are in the whirlpool:

— Feeling you are falling apart.
— Feeling you are going crazy.
— Your whole body shakes.
— Feeling of disorientation.
— Feeling of total confusion.
— Feeling you are disappearing.
— Feeling you are in limbo, knowing the old perceptions don't work yet not seeing any alternative.
— Feeling totally abandoned and alone.

— Feeling out of control.

— Feeling that no one cares or loves you.

These experiences happen when you are in the middle of the whirlpool and it is important that we see this as part of the transition from the old self to the discovery of the Real Self.

A Course in Miracles gives a clear description of this whirlpool experience, "The bridge [whirlpool] itself is nothing more than a transition in the perspective of reality. On this side, everything you see is grossly distorted and completely out of perspective. In the transition there is a period of confusion, in which a sense of actual disorientation may occur. But fear it not, for it means only that you have been willing to let go your hold on the distorted frame of reference that seemed to hold your world together. Fear not that you will be lifted up abruptly and hurled into reality. Time is kind, and if you use it on behalf of reality [Real Self], it will keep gentle pace with you in your transition. The urgency is only in dislodging your mind from its fixed position here. This will not leave you homeless and without a frame of reference. The period of disorientation, which precedes the actual transition, if far shorter than the time it took to fix your mind so firmly on illusions."*

To help ourselves through the whirlpool experience means having tools at our disposal to help us stay centered.

---

*A Course in Miracles, *Foundation for Inner Peace*, Box 1104, Glen Ellen, CA 95442, *text*, 1st ed.: p. 322; 2nd ed.: p. 346.

Some suggestions are:

(a) Meditation.

(b) Learning a relaxation exercise to use during the confusing times.

(c) Writing. Whenever you are in the whirlpool, sit down and write what you are feeling and thinking and you will drain off the anxieties and become centered.

(d) Draw, paint or use clay. These give the feelings another outlet and also lower the anxiety level and move us toward being centered.

In addition to these suggestions it can be helpful to have a person who can be a guide and centering point for you as you go through the whirlpool. This is part of my role as a psychotherapist. The following is an illustration I share with the people I see to help them understand the role I play in their change process.

Picture yourself standing and looking off to your left and there before you is your old self (the chicken), the self that is unhappy and tired of doing something that doesn't work, a self you would like to release and let go. Imagine me as your therapist standing beside you and asking you to look to your right and see your Real Self (the eagle), the way you were intended to be. You look back at me with a puzzled expression. "I don't see anything but a dense fog; I don't see anything there." But I reply, "No, you don't see it now but take my word for it, your Real Self is there." Now you are in a dilemma. You look to the left again, seeing the old self and knowing it's there, then looking to the right and seeing only a fog and hearing me say, "It's there." What are you to do? To move to the right is risky but you decide to go on, even though you see the whirlpool ahead. This is an act of faith. You venture forth into the fog and when the fear becomes overwhelming, you give me a call and we talk. You share your feelings of fear, anger or guilt, your fog level decreases and I again remind you that the Real Self is there. You feel centered again, also realizing that the fear didn't have the power over you that you thought it had. The whirlpool was not an endless experience. It is important to have a person who can help us keep centered as we go through this part of the change process.

A very important perception to have during this stage is that every situation, experience, or person is our teacher; whatever is happening is giving us feedback about ourselves. If we can perceive our experiences as teachers, not enemies or something to fear, we will be able to move through the emotional fog, the whirlpool, with a positive attitude, knowing that the experience is part of our growing and expanding.

Thirteen years ago when I was in the parish ministry, I went through a divorce and at that time divorced ministers were not in demand. Not only was my marriage going down the tube, but so was my career. This was my first whirlpool experience. At that time I was seeing a therapist. I'll never forget what he told me one day as I was falling apart in front of him, telling him how tragic my life was at that time. He told me what I was experiencing (the whirlpool) was not tragedy. Seeing my confused response, he went on to say, "The events of life are neutral and tragedy is when you allow the events of life to stop you from continuing to fulfill the person you were created to be and you start dying . . . and that's tragedy." "Now," he said, "You have two events in your life: your divorce and your career. You have a choice: you can either sit there, wallow in them or you can go through them, learn from them, grow from them and come out on the other end a more open, honest and aware person."

Seeing every experience as a teacher is a way of perceiving the whirlpool experience in a positive light. Even though the whirlpool experience is unpleasant, the two factors that sustain us through it are: seeing it as a source of learning about ourselves and knowing that it is part of the overall process of change.

STEP VI. FREEDOM FROM FALSE PERCEPTIONS

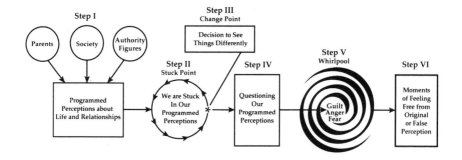

This is the moment of breakthrough. Having been in the whirlpool and feeling it is an endless experience, we see a moment of light. We have broken through the illusion of ongoing fear, just for an instant, but a Holy Instant of remembering some ancient truth that tells who and what we really are. Seeing the light of truth is a moment-by-moment unfoldment because too much light would blind us. As *A Course in Miracles* puts it: "Prisoners bound with heavy chains for years, starved and emaciated, weak and exhausted, and with eyes so long cast down in darkness they remember not the light, do not leap up in joy the instant they are made free. It takes a while for them to understand what freedom is."* This Holy Instant tells us that the whirlpool experience is only part of the process of coming into the light of truth. These moments of being free from

---

*A Course in Miracles, *Foundation for Inner Peace, Box 1104, Glen Ellen, CA 95442, text,* 1st ed.: pp. 401, 402; 2nd ed.: p. 431.

the false perception happen over and over until we have broken through the whirlpool so many times that we no longer fear the experience. Each moment of freedom and light gives us a growing assurance that the darkness of fear, anger and guilt has no more power over us.

STEP VII. FREEDOM TO HEAR OUR INNER CREATIVITY

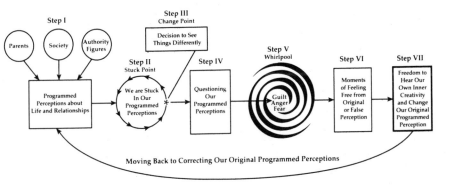

As we break through the whirlpool and experience our momentary points of freedom, we become open to hearing our own inner creativity telling us the truth about ourselves and our situation. With the freedom to hear our inner creativity (the eagle within) we can begin to correct the original false perceptions about ourselves—the chicken philosophy. This is illustrated by the line moving from Step VII back to Step I. The steps in our change process are now complete. We have started the process of correction.

Chapter V

An Overview of the Change Process

The diagram describes the overall process of changing our perception. The knowledge of these steps helps us see the whole experience in a positive light. The diagram also describes an experience that happens many times. You do not go through all of the steps and then become completely changed. Change takes place only in a moment. There is no other place where change happens except in a moment in time. There will be times when you choose to go through this process and at that moment you are changed. The next moment is not changed; that is another choice. There will be moments you decide to change and moments you decide not to change.

But overall change comes from the accumulation of changed moments. The momentary choices of moving from the programmed perception (the chicken philosophy) to being open to your inner creativity (the eagle philosophy) will happen many times and the accumulation of these momentary choices will expand into a corrected perception of ourselves. We will discover in the process that change is only choosing to make corrections in perception.

Another point to remember is that the first time through the change process is the most difficult because our survival of the whirlpool feels unsure. But once we have gone through the steps the first time and have experienced that moment of freedom, there is an inner knowing that tells us we are on the right path and gives us the strength to go through the process as often as is needed for the corrections to be made.

As we go through the change process we will still find ourselves operating under the chicken philosophy, but this is not regression. Rather, we now have continuous opportunities to choose again and make corrections. The more we go through the change process and expand our moments of freedom, the clearer we become about how deeply the chicken philosophy is ingrained in our being. Even though we continue to make the same errors, this is not a time to be hard on ourselves . . . but to see that each error is an opportunity to choose again and make a correction.

As the change process continues, we can become frustrated because there seem to be so many things to change and they just keep coming up. The only reason for this recurrence is to give us the opportunity to make corrections. The important thing is not how much keeps coming up but are we persistent, like the snail, in making our corrections?

Let me use an illustration to describe this point. Picture yourself drawing a straight line on a map between New York and San Francisco. This will be the flight path of an airplane taking off from New

York flying to San Francisco. Because of wind currents and weather, the airplane will not keep directly on the line but when it is in error, or off the flight path, the plane will correct—which becomes the next error which it corrects, which becomes the next error which is corrected, etc. So the only time we are truly on course is that moment in the zigzag when we actually cross the true path. Ninety percent of the way the airplane is off course . . . but it gets there.

Trying to follow the eagle philosophy, being on the line, is not as important as making momentary corrections and choices when the chicken philosophy raises its ugly head. Making those corrections keeps us close to the path and we finally reach our goal of a corrected perception about ourselves.

Another factor that may arise is our impatience in wanting the change to happen rapidly. All of us have been raised in a society based on the installment plan. Get it now, pay for it later. This is not the way of change; the opposite is true. You put forth the effort first and the results come later. Being consistently persistent in going through the process is one of the keys to gaining the results.

This leads us to another point. How do we know if change is happening and the process is working? Some clues to look for are the following:

— Decreasing of intensity while in the whirlpool.
— Diminishing of the amount of time spent in the whirlpool experience.

— An increase in the use of the suggested tools for going through the whirlpool.
— An increase in making corrections.
— An increase in the feeling of freedom.
— Feeling of being stuck diminishing.
— Beginning to see your life or situation differently.
— Beginning to feel inner peace.

As you continue to go through the process there will be a point at which you accept the process as a part of your ongoing expansion and growth. You will begin to see yourself moving back your limits, seeing things differently, feeling free and peaceful. In the very beginning the change process was strange and fearful; now you see the process in a positive light—not with fear, but a way of moving more blocks, fear, anger, and guilt, out of the way to discover the real truth about yourself.

As the eagle begins to unfold inside of us, we may remember the chicken yard with nostalgia and find ourselves revisiting it many times as we continue to correct our perceptions, but we now know that we will not continue to lead the life of a chicken because we have seen and experienced ourselves as who we really are—an eagle.

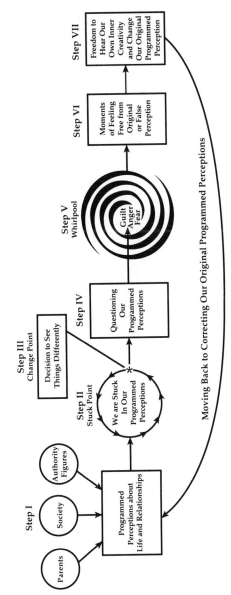

DIAGRAM OF THE CHANGE PROCESS

CONCLUSION

At this point let me suggest that you go back to the front of the book and re-read the story of the chicken and the eagle. This is the story of our path home, the discovery of who and what we really are. We have a choice and the choice is very simple: the chicken philosophy or the eagle philosophy; the choice of love or fear; the choice of going up empty tunnels or choosing the tunnel with the cheese; the choice of living in a barnyard or soaring in the heavens. Which will it be?

BIBLIOGRAPHY

A *Course in Miracles*. Foundation for Inner Peace: P.O. Box 1104, Glen Ellen, CA. 95442.

Bach, Richard. *Illusions*. Delacorte Press: New York, NY.

Boyd, Malcolm. *Book of Days*. Random House, 1968.

Emery, Stewart. *Actualizations*. Doubleday & Co., Inc.: Garden City, NY.

Frederick, Carl. *Playing the Game the New Way*. Delta Publishing Co., Inc.: New York, NY.

Joy, W. Brugh. *Joy's Way*. J.P. Tarcher, Inc.: Los Angeles, CA.

Paulson, J. Sig. *Your Power To Be*. Doubleday & Co., Inc.: Garden City, NY.

Wapnick, Kenneth. *Christian Psychology in A Course in Miracles*. Foundation for a Course in Miracles: Roscoe, NY.

MR. JERRY FANKHAUSER, M.S.W., is in private practice as a psychotherapist in Houston, Texas. Along with doing individual, marital, and family therapy, he also conducts workshops in the area of personal growth and development. He is a member of the American Association of Marriage and Family Therapists and the National Association of Social Workers.

Mr. Fankhauser has written four other books, *Everybody is Your Teacher, The Power of Affirmations, The Way of The Eagle* and *The Process of Waking Up.* In his writings and his practice, Mr. Fankhauser brings together the spiritual and psychological aspects of the person and sees the result of this merger to be spiritual psychotherapy.

If you wish to contact the author personally, he may be reached at the following address:

Mr. Jerry Fankhauser
7676 Woodway, Suite 160
Houston, Texas 77063
(713) 787-9057

All of Mr. Fankhauser's books can be obtained from your local bookstore or by ordering from:

De Vorss & Co.
P.O. Box 550
Marina del Ray, California 90294
(213) 870-7478